Routledge Revivals

Some Phases in the Life of Buddha

First published in 1915, this book presents a dramatization of part of Edwin Arnold's *The Light of Asia*. The original text represents one of the first successful attempts to popularise Buddhism and its founder Gautama Buddha — presenting his life, teachings and philosophy in verse poetry. This adaptation includes staging instructions, properties required, illustrative drawings of suggested costumes, and incidental music composed specifically for the piece. This book will be of interest to students of Indian and Buddhist literature — and how this has interacted with the West — as well as students of drama.

Some Phases in the Life of Buddha

Taken from 'The Light of Asia'

Edwin Arnold

Routledge
Taylor & Francis Group

First published in 1915
by Kegan Paul, Trench, Trübner & Co.

This edition first published in 2017 by Routledge
2 Park Square, Milton Park, Abingdon, Oxon, OX14 4RN
and by Routledge
711 Third Avenue, New York, NY 10017

Routledge is an imprint of the Taylor & Francis Group, an informa business

Publisher's Note

The publisher has gone to great lengths to ensure the quality of this reprint but points out that some imperfections in the original copies may be apparent.

Disclaimer

The publisher has made every effort to trace copyright holders and welcomes correspondence from those they have been unable to contact.

ISBN 13: 978-1-138-29010-5 (hbk)
ISBN 13: 978-1-315-26637-4 (ebk)
ISBN 13: 978-1-138-29028-0 (pbk)

King Suddhôdana and his Councillors

Frontispiece]

THE LIGHT OF ASIA Dramatised

SOME PHASES IN THE LIFE OF BUDDHA

TAKEN FROM

THE LIGHT OF ASIA

BY

SIR EDWIN ARNOLD

ARRANGED BY

VALERIE WYNGATE

WITH INCIDENTAL MUSIC BY

HUBERT BATH

AND FOUR ILLUSTRATIONS BY

RUPERT GODFREY LEE

Printed by BALLANTYNE, HANSON & CO.
at the Ballantyne Press, Edinburgh, Scotland

LIST OF ILLUSTRATIONS

NOTE ON THE COSTUME-DRAWINGS

THE costumes for these drawings are taken mostly from the Amaravati Tope carvings in the British Museum. They are intended to represent very roughly the dress of the earlier Indian period, which is quite unlike the modern. Much alteration has been necessary to adapt them to the requirements of private performance at a girls' school, though they are archæologically correct, and maintain, as far as possible, the spirit and particular characteristics of their period.

Further information as to the costumes can be had by studying the carvings placed on the great stairway of the British Museum.

RUPERT GODFREY LEE.

THE FOUR TRUTHS

Sorrow
Sorrow's Cause
Sorrow's Ceasing
The Way

THE EIGHT PRECEPTS

Right Doctrine
Right Purpose
Right Discourse
Right Behaviour
Right Purity
Right Thought
Right Lowliness
Right Rapture

THE SCENERY

THE simplest and most effective stage-setting is one consisting of curtains (velvet or serge in any dark colour that makes a good background)—one large curtain which covers the two sides and back of stage ; a second (smaller) curtain, which divides the stage in half, and which can be raised and lowered when necessary, thus :

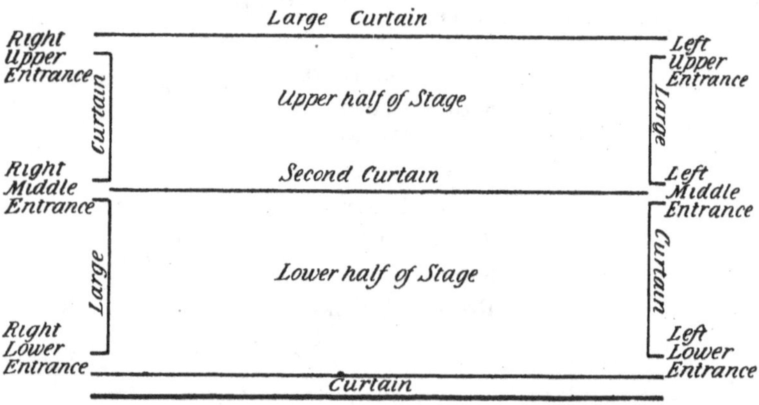

As seen above, there are six entrances—three on each side, none in the centre. The upper half of the stage is set permanently with divan, screen, brass bowl with flowers, and brasier containing burning incense. Both halves of the stage are used for all scenes played in Prince Siddârtha's Palace—viz. II, IV, VI. Scenes I, III, V are played, and "Chorus" reads his speeches, before the second curtain.

As the upper half of the stage remains set during the entire performance, and the second curtain is used whenever another scene is wanted, the action of the play is continuous; there need be no waits, and the curtain is lowered after:

First Chorus.
First Scene. Once during First Scene.
Third Chorus.
Third Scene.
Sixth Scene, and after Tableau.

The second curtain is lowered after:

Second Scene.
Fourth Scene.

After the Fifth Scene there is no curtain. The actors exeunt, leaving the stage empty.

If possible, the auditorium should be kept in darkness thoughout the play.

STAGE DIRECTIONS

R. U. E. . . .	Right upper entrance.
R. M. E. . . .	Right middle entrance.
R. L. E. . . .	Right lower entrance.
L. U. E. . . .	Left upper entrance.
L. M. E. . . .	Left middle entrance.
L. L. E. . . .	Left lower entrance.
R. C.	Right centre.
L. C.	Left centre.
D. R.	Down right.
D. L.	Down left.
X. R.	Crosses right.
X. L.	Crosses left.
X. C.	Crosses centre.
C.	Centre.

PROPERTIES REQUIRED

Scroll, electric light and battery for " Chorus " reader

THE actor who reads " Chorus " should be dressed in black draperies. In his hand he carries an electric light, hidden from the audience by the scroll from which he reads. Thus only his face is illuminated, care being taken that during the " Chorus " lines the stage and auditorium are in complete darkness. The electric battery can easily be carried under the reader's draperies.

SCENE I

Scroll for PRINCE.
Swan for PRINCE.
Emerald necklet for PRINCE.
Tray of gifts for COUNSELLOR.

SCENE II

Fans, cushions for ATTENDANTS.
Gourd.
Incense.
Bowl of flowers.

SCENE III

Earthenware bowl for PRINCE.
Pipes and drums for DANCERS.
Crystal bowl for SUJATA.

SCENE IV

Change of flowers for bowl.
Jewels for CHITRA (which she gives to MERCHANTS).

CHARACTERS

PRINCE SIDDÂRTHA
SAGE ACHARYA
SERVANT
KING SUDDHÔDANA
COUNSELLOR
YASÔDHARA
CHITRA
CHANNA
YOGI
KISAGÔTAMI
GOATHERD
SUJATA
RAHULA
TRIPUSHA } *Merchants*
BHALLUK }
FIRST COURTIER
SECOND COURTIER
ATTENDANTS
NAUTCH GIRLS

SOME PHASES IN THE LIFE OF BUDDHA

FIRST CHORUS

After the curtain rises and the auditorium is in darkness, READER *enters L. M. E. and stands C., in front of second curtain.*

The Scripture of the Saviour of the World,
Lord Buddha—Prince Siddârtha styled on earth—
In Earth and Heavens and Hells Incomparable,
All-honoured, Wisest, Best, most Pitiful ;
The Teacher of Nirvâna and the Law.

Thus came he to be born again for men.

Below the highest sphere four Regents sit
Who rule our world ; and under them are zones
Nearer, but high, where saintliest spirits dead
Wait thrice ten thousand years, then live again ;
And on Lord Buddha, waiting in that sky,
Came for our sakes the five sure signs of birth,
So that the Devas knew the signs, and said
' Buddha will go again to help the world.'
' Yea ! ' spake He, ' now I go to help the World
This last of many times ; for birth and death
End hence for me and those who learn my Law.

PRINCE :

(*Spoken to music.*)

Softly the Indian night sinks on the plains [*Music cue.*
At full moon in the month of Chaitra Shud,
When mangoes redden and the asoka buds
Sweeten the breeze, and Rama's birthday comes,
[*Rises.*] And all the fields are glad and all the towns.
And the moon swung above the western peaks,

And on a day found fortunate, the Prince
Took up his slate of ox-red sandal-wood
All beautiful by gems around the rim,
And sprinkled smooth with dust of emery,
These took he, and his writing-stick, and stood
With eyes bent down before the sage.
And thus until his eighteenth year they worked
Until the Prince had reached to man's estate.

[READER *extinguishes his light and exits L. M. E.*

CURTAIN.

SCENE I

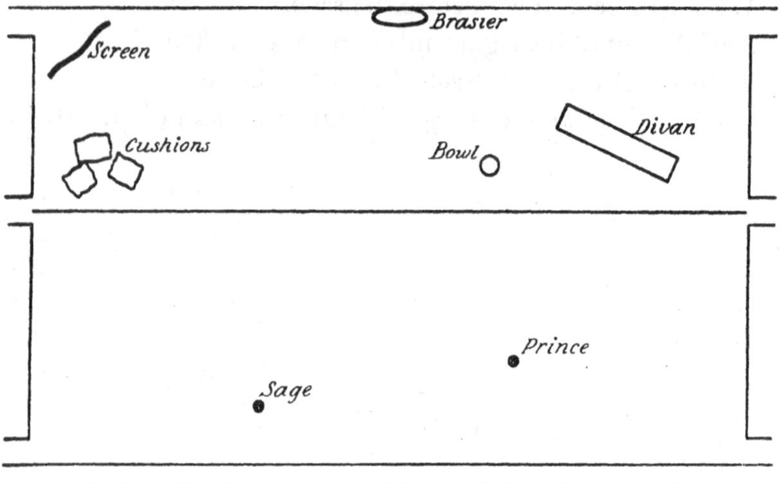

SIDDÂRTHA, SAGE ACHARYA, *discovered.* PRINCE *reading scroll. Offers scroll to* SAGE.

SAGE : (*taking scroll*)

'Tis good and rightly done, most noble Prince,
If these thou know'st needs it that I should teach
The mensuration of the lineal ?

PRINCE :

Be pleased to hear me. Paramanus ten
A parasukshma make ; ten of those build

The trasarene, and seven trasarenes
One mote's length floating in the beam, seven motes
The whisker point of mouse, and ten of these
One likhya ; likhyas ten a yuka, ten
Yukas a heart of barley, which is held
Seven times a wasp-waist,
And if it please
I shall recite how many sun-motes lie
From end to end within a yôjana.

[SAGE *prostrates himself before the* PRINCE.

SAGE :

For thou—thou, not I
Art Teacher of thy teachers—thou, not I
Art gurū. Oh, I worship thee, sweet Prince !
That comest to my school only to show
Thou knowest all without the books, and knowest
Fair reverence besides.

[*Looking off.*

A flock of wild swans passed, voyaging north,
To their rest-places on Himala's breast.
Calling in love-notes, down their snowy line
The bright birds flew, by fond love piloted ;

[*A swan pierced by an arrow falls at the* PRINCE'S *feet. He takes it up and smooths its feathers, seeing that it still lives. Swan falls on stage L. M. E. above* PRINCE, *so that he masks the bird from the audience.*

(*Enter* SERVANT, *L. L. E.*)

SERVANT : (*bowing*)

My Prince hath shot
A swan, which fell among the roses here,
He bids me pray you send it. Will you send ?

PRINCE :

Nay. That will I not. If the bird were dead
To send it to the slayer might be well,
But the swan lives ; my cousin hath but killed
The god-like speed which throbbed in its white wing.

SERVANT :

But Devadatta doth think the wild thing,
Living or dead, is his who fetched it down.
'Twas no man's in the clouds, but fall'n 'tis his.

PRINCE :

Say no ! the bird is mine,
The first of myriad things which shall be mine
By right of mercy and love's lordliness.
Say that to him. But if the Prince disputes
Let him submit his matter to the wise
And we will wait his word. (*To* SAGE.) Acharya, speak !

SAGE : (*X. L. of* PRINCE)

If life be aught, the saviour of a life
Owns more the living thing than he can own
Who sought to slay—the slayer spoils and wastes,
The cherisher sustains ; leave him (*pointing to* PRINCE) the swan :

[SERVANT *exits L. L. E.*

Prince Siddartha and the Swan

To face page 6]

(*Enter* KING SUDDHÔDANA *with* COUNSELLOR, *R. M. E.*)

KING:

Come,
Sweet son! and see the pleasaunce of the spring,
And how the fruitful earth is wooed to yield
Its riches to the reaper; how my realm—
Which shall be thine when the pile flames for me—
Feeds all its mouths and keeps the King's chest filled.
Fair is the season with new leaves, bright blooms,
Green grass, and cries of plough time.

[KING *and* PRINCE *exeunt R. M. E.* PRINCE *carries swan off, and leaves it in the wings.*

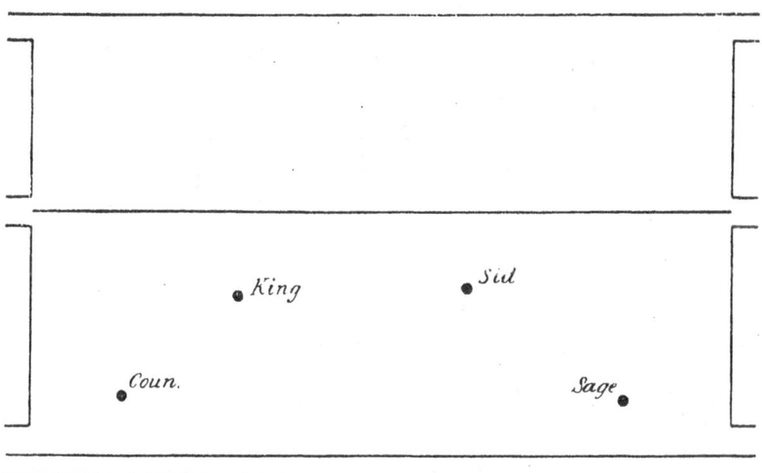

SAGE: (*L. C., speaking to* COUNSELLOR, *D. R.*)

See how they ride
Into a land of wells and gardens where
The pied king-fishers hang; in mango-sprays

The sun-birds flash ; alone at his green forge
Toils the loud coppersmith ; bee-eaters hawk,
Chasing the purple butterflies ; beneath
Striped squirrels race, the mynas perk and pick,
The blue doves coo from every well, far off
The village drums beat for some marriage feast ;

[*Re-enter* KING *and* PRINCE *R. M. E.* KING *enters after* PRINCE.

KING : (*R. C.*)

All things spoke peace and plenty, and the Prince
Saw and rejoiced.

PRINCE : (*C.*)

But looking deep, I saw
The thorns which grow upon this rose of life :
How the swart peasant sweated for his wage,
Toiling for leave to live ; and how he urged
The great-eyed oxen through the flaming hours,
Goading their velvet flanks ; then marked I, too,
How lizard fed on ant, and snake on him,
And kite on both ; and how the fish-hawk robbed
The fish-tiger of that which it had seized ;
The shrike chasing the bulbul, which did hunt
The Jewelled butterflies ; till everywhere
Each slew a slayer and in turn was slain,
Life living upon death. So the fair show
Veiled one vast, savage, grim conspiracy
Of mutual murder, from the worm to man,
Who himself kills his fellow.
(*To* KING, *sighing.*) Is this

That happy earth they brought me forth to see ?
How salt will sweat the peasant's bread, how hard
The oxen's service ! in the brake how fierce
The war of weak and strong ! i' th' air what plots.
No refuge e'en in water. Go aside
A space, and let me muse on what ye show.

[He exits L. M. E.

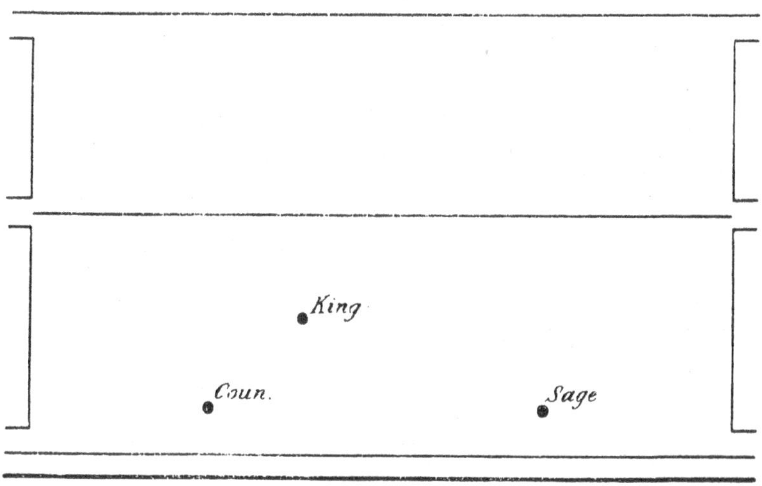

KING :

Bethink ye, Sirs ! how the old Rishi spake.
Remember what my dream-readers foretold.
This boy, more dear to me than mine own heart's blood,
Shall be of universal dominance,
Trampling the neck of all his enemies,
A king of kings—and this is in my heart ;—
Or shall he tread the sad and lowly path
Of self-denial and of pious pains,

Gaining who knows what good, when all is lost
Worth keeping ; and to this his wistful eyes
Do still incline amid my palaces.
But ye are sage, and ye will counsel me ;
How may his feet be turned to that proud road
Which gave him Earth to rule, if he would rule ?

SAGE :

Maharaja ! love
Will cure these thin distempers ; weave the spell
Of woman's wiles about his idle heart.
The thoughts ye cannot stay with brazen chains
A girl's hair lightly binds.

COUNSELLOR :

All that is just ; but if we seek him wives,
Love chooseth ofttimes with another eye ;

SAGE :

Do this, my King ! command a festival
Where the realm's maids shall be competitors
In youth and grace, and sports that Sakyas use.
Let the Prince give the prize to the fair,
And, when the lovely victors pass his seat,
There shall be those who mark if one or two
Change the fixed sadness of his tender cheek ;

KING :

So may we choose for Love with Love's own eyes.

SAGE :

And cheat his Highness into happiness.

KING:

This thing seems good. Wherefore command to-day
The criers bid the young and beautiful
Pass to the palace, for 'tis in command
To hold a court of pleasure, and the Prince
Will give the prizes, something rich for all,
The richest for the fairest judged. [*Music cue.*

[COUNSELLOR *exits R. M. E. Curtain descends; rises immediately.*

[*Positions as curtain rises.* MAIDENS *enter L. M. E. Bow to* KING; *X. R. to* PRINCE; *receives gift; group themselves at back of stage.*

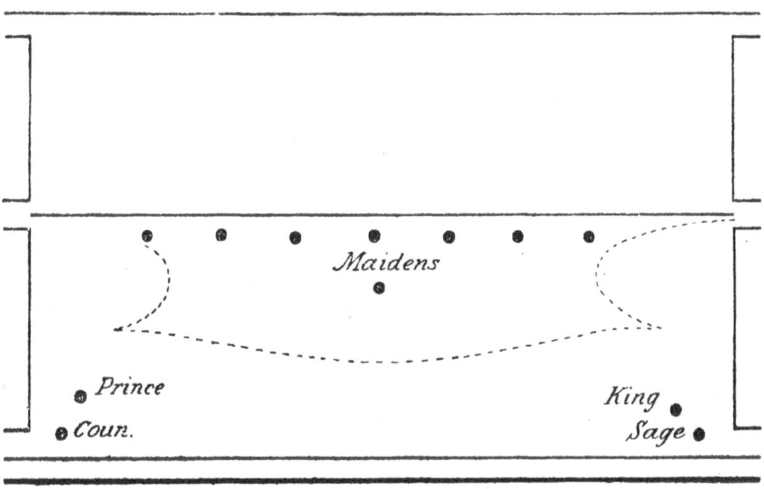

As Maidens *pass before* King *and* Prince, *the following music is played. The music stops at* Yasôdhara's *speech, 'Is there a gift for me.'*

dim.
p dolce espressio.
p
dim. rall.
tr
pp
dim.
pp

(YASÔDHARA *enters L. M. E.; goes towards* PRINCE. *She does not bow to* KING, *and remains standing in the centre of the stage.*)

YASÔDHARA :

Is there a gift for me ? [*Music stops.*

PRINCE :

The gifts are gone that I would give, yet take
This for amends, dear sister, of whose grace,
Our happy city boasts ;
[*Takes emerald necklet from his throat, clasps it round her waist*; *to L. of* YASÔDHARA.
My Sweet, we were not strangers, as to us
And all it seemed ; in ages long gone by
A hunter's son, playing with forest girls
By Yamun's springs, where Nandadevi stands,
Sat umpire while they raced beneath the firs
Like hares at eve that run their playful rings ;
One with flower-stars he crowned ; one with long plumes,
One with fir-apples ; but who ran the last
Came first for him, and unto her the boy
Gave a tame fawn and his heart's love beside.
And in the wood they lived many glad years,
And in the wood they undivided died.
And I was he and she Yasôdhara ;
And while the wheel of birth and death turns round,
That which hath been must be between us two.

YASÔDHARA : (*R. C.*)

Dear Prince, behold me who am wholly thine.

[YASÔDHARA *and* PRINCE *walk up stage; stand C., with their backs towards the audience.*

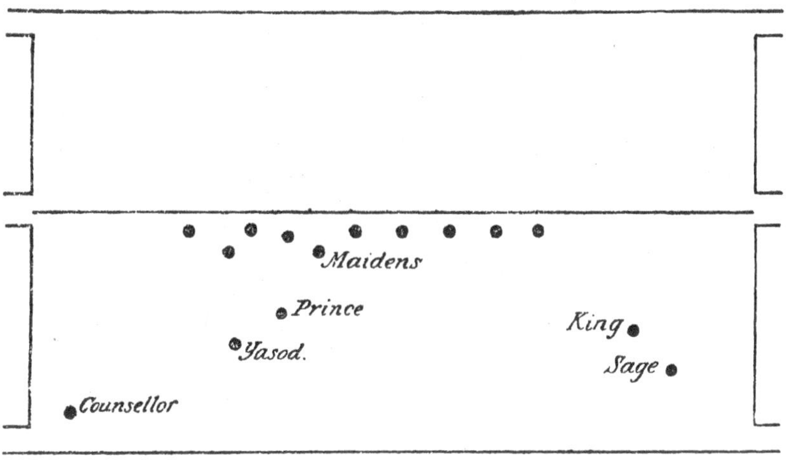

KING :

Look! we have found a lure! (*To* SAGE.) Take counsel now
To fetch herewith our falcon from the clouds.
Let messengers be sent to ask the maid
In marriage for my son.

SAGE :

My King, do not forget that it is law
With Sakyas, when any ask a maid
Of noble house, fair and desirable,
He must make good his skill in martial arts,
Against all suitors who should challenge it,
Nor might this custom break itself for Kings.

PRINCE : (*coming down stage with* YASÔDHARA)

To you all I say—this, too, I have learned ;
[*To* KING.] Make proclamation that thy son will meet
All-comers at their chosen games. I think
I shall not lose my love for such as these.

END SCENE I

CURTAIN

SECOND CHORUS

Curtain rises. READER *enters as before, L. M. E. Stands C., in front of second curtain.*

Now, as our Lord was come to eighteen years,
The King commanded that there should be built
Three stately houses, one of hewn square beams
With cedar lining, warm for winter days ;
One of veined marbles, cool for summer heat ;
And one of burned bricks, with blue tiles bedecked
Pleasant at seed time, when the champaks bud
And night and day served there a chosen band
Of nautch girls, cup-bearers, and cymballers,
Delicate dark-browed ministers of love
Who fanned the sleeping eyes of the happy prince,
And when he waked, led back his thoughts to bliss
With music whispering through the blooms, and charm
Of amorous songs, and dreamy dances, linked
By chime of ankle-bells and wave of arms
And silver vina-strings ; while essences
Of musk and champak, and the blue haze spread
From burning spices, soothed his soul again
To drowse by sweet Yasôdhara ; and thus
Siddârtha lived forgetting.
                                        Furthermore
Bright-eyed attendants watched to execute

Sentence on such as spake of the harsh world
Without, where aches and plagues were, tears and fears
And wail of mourners, and grim fume of pyres.
'Twas treason if a thread of silver strayed
In tress of singing-girl or nautch-dancer ;
And every dawn the dying rose was plucked,
The dead leaves hid, all evil sights removed :

Wherefore, around that pleasant prison-house—
Where love was jailer and delights its bars
But far removed from sight, the King bade build
A massive wall, and in the wall a gate
With brazen folding-doors, and through all these
Must one pass if he quit the pleasure house.
Three mighty gates there were, bolted and barred,
And over each was set a faithful watch,
And the King's order said, ' Suffer no man
To pass the gates, though he should be the Prince.
This on your lives—even though it be my son.'

In which calm home of happy life and love
Lived our Lord Buddha, knowing not of woe,
Nor want, nor pain, nor plague, nor age, nor death.

[*Music cue.*

[READER *exits L. M. E. The stage and auditorium are in total darkness. The second curtain is down.*

'CELLO.
PIANO.
Andante. mf
dolce
Andante.
mf
Ped.
Ped.
Ped.
sempre arpeggiando

mf
f

dim.
p
mp
pp
8va
mp
pp
Ped.

We are the voices of the wandering wind, Which moan for rest, and rest can never find;
8va.
p
Lo! as the wind is, so is mortal life, A moan, a sigh, a sob, a storm, a strife.
8va.
pp
O Maya's son! because we roam the earth Moan we upon these strings;

We make no mirth, So many woes we see in many lands.
So many streaming eyes and wringing hands.
mf
tr
But thou that art to save thine hour is nigh ! The sad world waiteth in its misery,
cres.
The blind world stumbleth on its round of pain.
Rise, Maya's child ! wake ! slumber not again !
Ped.

mf
3
dim.
pp
5
8va
mf
We are the voices of the wandering wind ; Wander thou too, O Prince, thy rest to find ;
8va
5
Leave love for love of lovers, for woe's sake, Quit state for sorrow, and deliverance make.

[*For " The Voices of the Wind"—the more voices heard in these lines the better the effect obtained. The words should be intoned or chanted. In order to give the required air of mystery, the auditorium should be in darkness, and the actors who speak these lines should stand behind the second curtain (which is lowered). At the end of the chant the second curtain rises and Scene II begins. There should be no pause after the chant. The " Voices " music merging into the opening music for Scene II.*

VOICES OF THE WIND

(*Spoken to music.*)

We are the voices of the wandering wind,
Which moan for rest, and rest can never find ;
Lo ! as the wind is, so is mortal life,
A moan, a sigh, a sob, a storm, a strife.

O Maya's son ! because we roam the earth
Moan we upon these strings ; we make no mirth,
So many woes we see in many lands,
So many streaming eyes and wringing hands.

But thou that art to save, Thine hour is nigh ;
The sad world waiteth in its misery,
The blind world stumbleth on its round of pain.
Rise, Maya's child ! wake ! slumber not again.

We are the voices of the wandering wind ;
Wander thou too, O Prince, thy rest to find ;
Leave love for love of lovers, for woe's sake,
Quit state for sorrow, and deliverance make.

SCENE II

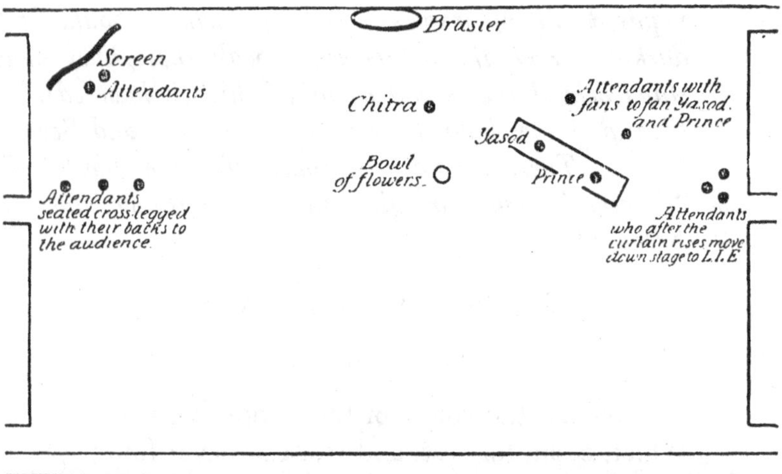

PRINCE SIDDÂRTHA'S *Court*. PRINCE SIDDÂRTHA, YASÔDHARA, CHITRA, COURTIERS, MAIDENS.

' *Softly the Indian night sinks on the plains.*' [*Music cue. Stops at* ' *And all the sleeping land.*'

dim.
p dolce espressio.

PRINCE :

(*Spoken to music.*)

Softly the Indian night sinks on the plains [*Music cue.*
At full moon in the month of Chaitra Shud,
When mangoes redden and the asoka buds
Sweeten the breeze, and Rama's birthday comes,
[*Rises.*] And all the fields are glad and all the towns.
And the moon swung above the western peaks,

Climbing the spangled vault, and lighting clear
Rohinis ripples, shows the hills and vales,
And all the sleeping land ; [*Music stops.*
[*To* ATTENDANT.]
Go bid the vinas sound ; and tell them set
A stringed gourd on the sill, there where the wind
Could linger o'er its notes and play at will.

[ATTENDANT, *sitting D. R., fetches gourd from off stage R. M. E. Crosses with gourd, in front of* PRINCE, *bows low, carries gourd off stage L. L. E.*

Wild music makes the wind on silver strings. (*Sits.*)

[*Wind sighs in the strings.*

[*One voice only should chant these two verses, clearly and slowly. The actor speaking the lines must stand in L. L. E., but not seen by the audience. Of the actors on the stage none hears the voice except the* PRINCE, *whose facial expression shows deep agitation.*

We are the voices of the wandering wind,
Which moan for rest, and rest can never find ;
Lo ! as the wind is, so is mortal life,
A moan, a sigh, a sob, a storm, a strife.

We are the voices of the wandering wind,
Wander thou too, O Prince, thy rest to find ;
Leave love for love of lovers, for woe's sake
Quit state for sorrow, and deliverance make.

PRINCE : (*starting up*)

My world ! Oh, world !
I hear ! I know ! I come !

YASÔDHARA : (*kneeling*)

What ails my Lord ? Siddârtha ! Well-belov'd !
Hath not my Lord still his gladness in me ?

PRINCE :

My Sweet ! Such gladness that my inmost soul
Aches, thinking it must end, for it will end,
And we shall both grow old, Yasôdhara,
Loveless, unlovely, weak and old, and bowed.
And all my heart is darkened with its dread,
And all my heart is fixed to think how love
Might save its sweetness from the slayer, Time,
Who makes men old. Enough ! (*Sighs.*) Let some maid tell
An ancient tale to speed the hour of dusk. [*Music cue.*

A. '*Speed the hour of dusk.*' *Music cue. Music stops at* '*Sank into seas.*'

B. '*Our brazen gates.*' *Music cue. Music stops at* '*Crores of folk.*'

con sord. mp dolce
Ped.
Ped.
Ped.
Ped.
Ped.
Ped.

Ped.
f
f
dim.

CHITRA :

Of love and of a magic horse, and lands
Wonderful, distant, where pale peoples dwelled,
And where the sun at night sank into seas. [*Music stops.*

PRINCE :

Chitra brings me back
The wind's song in the strings with that fair tale :
Give her, Yasôdhara, thy pearl for thanks.

[YASÔDHARA *does so.*

But thou, my pearl, is there so wide a world ?
Is there a land which sees the great sun roll
Into the waves, and are their hearts like ours,
Countless, unknown, not happy—it may be—
Whom we might succour if we knew of them ?
There must be many we should love—how else ?
O Chitra ! you that know of fairyland !
Where tether they that swift steed of thy tale ?

My palace for one day upon his back,
To ride and ride and see the spread of the earth ;
Nay, if I had yon callow vulture's plumes,
The carrion heir of wider realms than mine,
How would I stretch for topmost Himalay,
Light where the rose-gleam lingers on those snows,
And strain my gaze with searching what is round !
Why have I never seen and never sought ?
Tell me what lies beyond our brazen gates.

[*Music repeated.*

CHITRA :

(*To music.*)

The city first, fair Prince, and then there are
The Temples and the gardens, and the groves,
And then the fields ; and afterwards fresh fields.
With nullahs, maidâus, Jungle, koss on koss ;
And next King Bimbisâra's realm, and then
The vast flat world, with crores on crores of folk.

[*Music stops.*

PRINCE :

Good. Go. One of you! Let the word be sent
That Channa yoke my chariot—at noon.
To-morrow I shall ride and see beyond.

[*An* ATTENDANT *near screen bows before* PRINCE, *and exits R. M. E.*

[CHANNA *enters R. M. E., with* ATTENDANT.

CHANNA : (*bowing before* PRINCE)

Great Master, I am come!

PRINCE :

Bring thou my horse,
For now the hour is come when I should quit
This golden prison where my heart lives caged,
To find the truth ; which henceforth I will seek,
For all men's sake, until the truth be found.

CHANNA : (*stands C., below* PRINCE)

Alas! dear Prince,
Spake then for nought those wise and holy men
Who cast the stars and bade us wait the time
When King Suddhôdana's great son should rule
Realms upon realms, and be a Lord of Lords?
Wilt thou ride hence and let the rich world slip
Out of thy grasp to hold a beggar's bowl?
Wilt thou go forth into the friendless waste
That hast this Paradise of pleasures here?

PRINCE :

Unto this I came
And not for thrones : the kingdom that I crave
Is more than many realms, and all things pass
To change and death. Bring me forth Kantaka !

CHANNA :

Most honoured,
Bethink thee of my Lord thy father's grief !
Bethink thee of their woe whose bliss thou art.
How shalt thou help them, first undoing them ?

PRINCE :

Friend, that love is false
Which clings to love for selfish sweets of love ;
But I, who love these more than joys of mine—
Yea, more than joys of theirs—depart to save
Them and all flesh, if utmost love avail :
Go, bring me Kantaka !

CHANNA :

Master, I go.
[*Exits R. M. E.*

PRINCE :

I will depart. The hour is come. I go
As in the silence of the sky I read
My fated message flashing : unto this
Came I, and unto this all nights and days

Have led me ; for I will not have the crown
Which may be mine ; I lay aside these realms,
Which wait the gleaming of my naked sword :
My chariot shall not roll with bloody wheels,
From victory to victory, till earth
Wears the red record of my name.
I choose
To tread its paths with patient, stainless feet,
Making its dust my bed, its loneliest wastes
My dwelling, and its meanest things my mates.

SECOND CURTAIN.

THIRD CHORUS

READER *enters L. M. E., as before. Stands C. before second curtain.*

The Prince and Channa passed beyond the gates,
Which opened to the signet of the king ;
As they rode out Siddârtha turned and spake
Full sweet to Channa : ' This which thou hast done
Will bring thee good, and bring all creatures good ;
Be sure I love thee always for thy love,
Lead back my horse, and take my crest-pearl here,
My princely robes, which henceforth stead me not,
My jewelled sword.
Give the King all, and say
Siddârtha prays forget him till he come
Ten times a Prince, with royal wisdom won
From lonely searchings and the strife for light ;
Where, if I conquer, lo ! all earth is mine—
Mine by chief service !—tell him—mine by love !
Since there is hope for man only in man ;
And none hath sought for this as I will seek,
Who cast away my world to save my world.

Forth fared he by the common way alone ;
Mingling with all the Sâkya citizens,
Seeing the glad and sad things of the town ;

Siddârtha's farewell to Kantaka and Channa

To face page 38]

The painted streets alive with hum of noon ;
The buyers with their money in the cloth,
The war of words to cheapen this or that,
The shout to clear the road, the huge stone wheels,
The strong slow oxen with their rustling loads,
The singing bearers with the palanquins,
The dyers stretching waistcloths in the sun
Wet from the vats—orange, and rose, and green ;
The Brahman proud, the martial Kshatriya,
The humble toiling Sudra ; here a throng,
There a long line of drums and horns, which went,
With steeds gay painted and silk canopies,
To bring the young bride home.

Onward he passed,
Exceeding sorrowful, seeing how men
Fear so to die they are afraid to fear,
Lust so to live they dare not love their life,
But plague it with fierce penances, belike
To please the gods who grudge pleasure to man ;
Belike to baulk hell by self-kindled hells ;
Belike in holy madness, hoping soul
May break the better through their wasted flesh.

. . . .

Round Rajagriha five fair hills arose,
Guarding King Bimbisâra's sylvan town :
A winding track, paven with footworn slabs,
Leads on, by safflower fields, and bamboo tufts,
Low cliffs and flats of jungle-flowers, to where
The shoulder of the mountain, sloping west,
O'erhangs a cave with wild figs canopied ;
Lo ! thou who comest hither, bare thy feet

And bow thy head ! For all this spacious earth
Hath not a spot more dear and hallowed. Here
Lord Buddha sate the scorching summers through,
The driving rains, the chilly dawns and eves ;
Wearing for all men's sake the yellow robe,
Eating in beggar's guise the scanty meal
Chance gathered from the charitable ;
By day and night *there* dwelt the world-honoured,
Subduing that fair body born for bliss,
Thus would he muse from noon-tide—when the land
Shimmered with heat, and walls and temples danced
In the reeking air—till sunset, noting not
The blazing globe roll down, nor evening glide,
Purple and swift across the softened fields ;
Then slept he for what space the fleet moon asks
To swim a tenth part of her cloudy sea ;
When night was dead ; new day begun, our Lord,
After the manner of a Rishi, hailed
The rising orb, and went—ablutions made—
Down by the winding path unto the town ;
And in the fashion of a Rishi passed
From street to street, with begging-bowl in hand,
Gathering the little pittance of his needs.

And still our Lord went on, Teaching how fair
This earth were if all living things be linked
In friendliness and common use of foods,
Bloodless and pure ; the golden grain, bright fruits,
Sweet herbs which grow for all, the waters pure,
Sufficient drinks and meats. Which when they heard,
The might of gentleness so conquered them,

The priests themselves scattered their altar flames,
And flung away the steel of sacrifice,

. . . .

So passed our Lord away
Towards Uravilva, not yet comforted,
And wan of face, and weak with six years' quest.

. . . .

He westwards from the 'Thousand Gardens' went,
By Gunga's valley, till His steps were set
On the green hills where those twin streamlets spring,
Nilâjan and Mohâna ; both most fair.
There in the sylvan solitudes once more
Lord Buddha lived, musing the woes of men—
Sitting serene with perfect virtue walled
As is a stronghold by its gates ; and so
Our Lord attained *Sammâ-sambuddh ;* he saw,
By light which shines beyond our mortal ken,
The line of all his lives in all the worlds ;
Far back and farther back, and farthest yet,
How new life reaps what the old life did sow ;
How where its march breaks off its march begins ;
Holding the gain and answering for the loss ;
And how each life's good begets more good,
Evil fresh evil. Lo ! the world's great Dawn
Sprang with Buddh's victory ! Lo ! in the East
Flamed the first fires of beauteous day, poured forth
Through fleeting folds of night's black drapery.
Yea ! and so holy was the influence
Of that high Dawn which came from victory
That, far and near, in homes of men there spread

An unknown peace. The slayer hid his knife,
The robber laid his plunder back ; the shroff
Counted full tale of coins ; all evil hearts
Grew gentle, kind hearts gentler, as the balm
Of that divinest Daybreak lightened Earth.

[READER *exits, as before, L. M. E.*

CURTAIN.

SCENE III

SCENE : *A Road. This scene is played before the second curtain.*

Curtain rises. PRINCE SIDDÂRTHA *discovered, C., seated cross-legged in conventional 'Buddha' attitude.*

Ye ! suffering world ;
Oh ! known and unknown of my common flesh,
Caught in this common net of death and woe,
And life which binds to both ! I see, I feel
The vastness of the agony of earth,
The vainness of its joys, the mockery
Of all its best, the anguish of its worst ;
Me, too, this lure hath cheated, so it seemed
Lovely to live, and life a sunlit stream
For ever flowing in a changeless peace ;
Since pleasures end in pain the veil is rent
Which blinded me ! I am as all these men
Who cry upon their gods and are not heard,
Or are not heeded—yet there must be help !
Perchance the gods have need of help themselves,
Being so feeble that when sad lips cry
They cannot save. I would not let one cry
Whom I could save ! How can it be that Brahm
Would make a world, and keep it miserable,
Since, if all powerful, he leaves it so,

He is not good, and if not powerful,
He is not God ?—

(*Enter* Yogi, *L. M. E.*)

Prince : (*C.*)

Much-suffering Sir !
These many moons I dwell upon the hill—
Who am a seeker of the truth—and see
My brothers here, and thee, so piteously
Self-anguished ; wherefore add ye ills to life
Which is so evil ?

Yogi : (*L. C., crouching on the ground in front of* Prince)

'Tis written if a man shall mortify
His flesh, till pain be grown the life he lives
And death voluptuous rest, such woes shall purge
Sin's dross away, and the Soul, purified,
Soar from the furnace of its sorrow, winged
For glorious spheres and splendour past all thought.

Prince :

Yon cloud so luminous which floats in heaven,
[*Rises, points to sky.* Yogi *follows the movement with his eyes.*
Wreathed like gold cloth around your Indra's Throne,
Rose thither from the tempest-driven sea ;
But it must fall again in tearful drops
Trickling through rough and painful water-ways
To Gunga and the sea, wherefrom it sprang.

Know'st thou, my brother, if it be not thus,
After their many pains, with saints in bliss?
Since that which rises falls, and that which buys
Is spent; and if ye buy heaven with your blood
In Hell's hard market, when the bargain's through
The toil begins again!

YOGI: (*rises*)

It may begin. Alas! we know not this,
Nor surely anything; yet after night
Day comes, and after turmoil peace, and we
Hate this accursed flesh which clogs the soul
That fain would rise; so, for the sake of soul
Most rightly have we chosen this for road—
[*He crosses D. R.*
And tread it Rajaputra! till the close—
Though all its stones were fire—in trust of death.
Speak if thou know'st a way more excellent;
If not, peace go with thee! [*Exit* YOGI, *R. L. E.*

[*From the other side enters a woman,* KISAGÔTAMI, *young, tearful; salutes, bending low.*

KISAGÔTAMI: (*enters, L. M. E., and kneels, L. C.*)

Lord! Rishi! thou art he who yesterday
Had pity on me in the fig-grove here,
Where I live lone and reared my child; but he
Straying amid the blossoms found a snake
Which twined about his waist whilst he did laugh

And tease the quick-forked tongue and opened mouth
Of that cold playmate. But alas ! ere long
He turned so pale and still, I could not think
Why he should cease to play, and let my hand
Fall from his clasp. And one said, ' He is sick
Of poison ' ; and another, ' He will die.'
But I, who could not lose my precious boy,
Prayed of them physic which might bring the light
Back to his eyes ; it was so very small
The kiss-mark of the serpent, and I think
It could not hate him, gracious as he was,
Nor hurt him in his sport. And some one said,
There is a holy man upon the hill—
Lo ! now he passeth in the yellow robe—
Ask of the Rishi if there be a cure
For that which ails thy son. Whereupon I came
Trembling to thee, whose brow is like a god's,
Praying thee tell what simples might be good.
And thou, great Sir, didst spurn me not, but gaze
With gentle eyes and touch with patient hand ;
Then draw the face-cloth back, saying to me,

PRINCE : (*C.*)

Yea ! little Sister, there is that might heal.
Thee first, then him, if thou could'st fetch the thing ;
For they who seek physicians bring to them
What is ordained. Therefore, I pray thee, find
Black mustard-seed, a tola ; only mark
Thou take it not from any hand or house
Where father, mother, child, or slave hath died :

KISAGÔTAMI : (*L. C.*)

It will be well if thou can'st find the seed ;
Thus did'st thou speak, my Lord !

PRINCE :

Yea ! I spake thus,
Dear Kisagôtami. But didst thou find
The seed ?

KISAGÔTAMI :

I went, Lord, clasping to my breast
The babe, grown colder, asking at each hut—
' I pray you give me mustard, of your grace,
A tola—black ' ; and each who had it gave,
But when I asked, ' In my friend's household here
Hath any peradventure ever died—
Husband, or wife, or child, or slave ? ' they said :
O sister ! what is this you ask ? the dead
Are very many and the living few.
So with sad thanks I gave the mustard back,
And prayed of others, but the others said,
Here is the seed, but we have lost our slave !
Here is the seed, but our good man is dead !
Here is some seed, but he that sowed it, died
Between the rain-time and the harvesting !
Oh ! Sir ! I could not find a single house
Where there was mustard seed and none had died !
Therefore I left my child who would not play
Nor smile—beneath the wild vines by the stream, [*Rises.*
To seek thy face and kiss thy feet, and pray
Where I might find this seed and find no death,

If now indeed my baby be not dead,
As I do fear, and as they said to me.

PRINCE :

My Sister ! thou hast found—in thy deep grief
Searching for what none finds—that bitter balm
I had to give thee—He thou lovedst slept
Dead on thy bosom yesterday ; to-day
Thou know'st the whole wide world weeps with thy woe :
The grief which all hearts share grows less for one.
Lo ! I would pour my blood if it could stay
Thy tears and win the secret of that curse
Which makes sweet love our anguish, and which drives—
O'er flowers and pastures to the sacrifice—
As these dumb beasts are driven—men their lords.
I seek that secret :
Bury thou thy child.
[*Exit* KISAGÔTAMI, *L. L. E.*

[PRINCE *faints from weariness and want of food. Enter a* GOATHERD. *He comes to the* PRINCE *and offers to help him.*

(GOATHERD *enters R. L. E.*)

GOATHERD :

Ah, my Lord,
I cannot help thee, for thou see'st my caste—
I am a Sudra, and my touch defiles !

PRINCE :

[*During this speech* PRINCE *slowly moves into the R. upper corner of stage,* GOATHERD *following him.*

Pity and need
Make all flesh kin. There is no caste in blood,
Which runneth of one hue, nor caste in tears,
Which trickle salt with all and bring relief.
Give me to drink, my brother ; when I am come
Unto my quest it shall be good for thee.

[NAUTCH GIRLS' *music heard in the distance.* PRINCE *looks off L.*

'*It shall be good for thee.*' (*Music cue.*)

The lines on p. 56 are spoken through the first twelve bars of the dance music ; then the dancers enter.

The music should begin softly, increasing in loudness as the dancers approach.

INDIAN DANCE.

Andante grazioso.
mf
mf

Fine.
Vivo. mp
Vivo. mf

Repeat 4 times; then :𝄋: al fine.
3

PRINCE:

A band of tinselled girls, the Nautch dancers
Of Indra's temple in the town, with those
Who make their music—one that beats a drum
Set round with peacock-feathers, one that blows
The piping bansuli, and one that plays
A three-string sitar!
All the silver bells
Chiming soft peals about the small brown feet,
Armlets and wrist-rings tattling answer shrill;

[*Dancers enter L. M. E. They dance across the stage and exit R. L. E.*

DANCE.

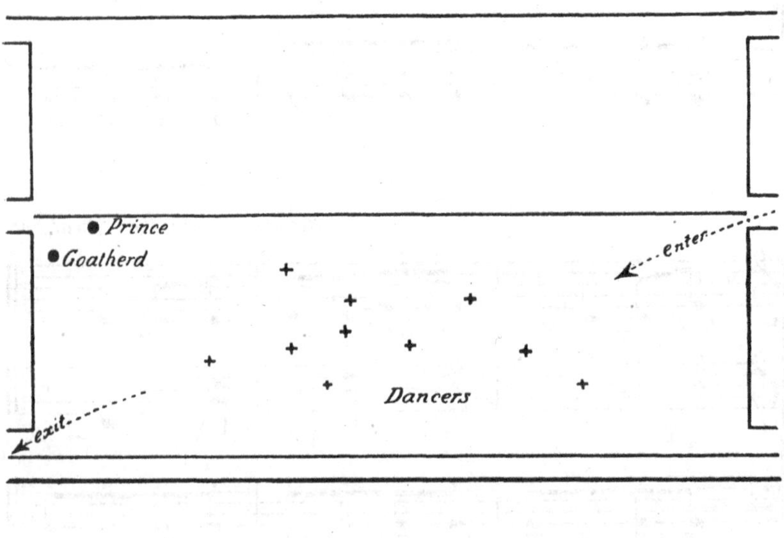

Song of the NAUTCH GIRLS.

(*These words are murmured during the dance by different dancers.*)

Fair goes the dancing when the sitar's tuned.
Tune us the sitar neither low nor high,
And we will dance away the hearts of men.

The string o'erstretched breaks, and the music flies,
The string o'erslack is dumb, and music dies;
Tune us the sitar neither low nor high.

PRINCE:

[PRINCE *rises and crosses D. R., looking off at departed dancers.*

Truly! the foolish ofttimes teach the wise;
I strain too much the string of life belike,
[*Goes to centre of stage.*
Meaning to make such music as shall save.
Mine eyes are dim now that they see the truth,
My strength is waned now that my need is most;
[*Sinks on his knees.*
Would that I had such help as man must have,
For I shall die, whose life was all men's hope.

[*Falls forward, with his head on his arms.* GOATHERD *comes to his assistance, and kneels R. C. at* PRINCE'S *feet. At* SUJATA'S *entrance* GOATHERD *moves D. L., and remains there during the rest of the scene.*

(SUJATA *enters R. L. E., carrying a bowl on her head. She draws near ; kisses the earth.*)

SUJATA :

Would that the Holy One
Inhabiting this grove, Giver of good,
Merciful unto me his handmaiden,
Vouchsafing now his presence, might accept
These our poor gifts of snowy curds, fresh made
With milk as white as new-carved ivory.

[*She pours the curds and milk into the bowl.*

PRINCE :

What is it that thou dost bring me ?

SUJATA :

Holy One]!
From our droves I took milk of a hundred—
And with that milk I fed fifty white cows,
That yield I boiled with sandal and fine spice
In silver lotas, adding rice, well grown
From chosen seed set in new-broken ground,
So picked that every grain was like a pearl.

[SUJATA *is L. C. and above* PRINCE *when she offers the bowl of milk.* PRINCE'S *back is turned towards audience while he drinks, and he returns* SUJATA *the bowl.*

PRINCE : (*rises*)

Long be thy bliss,
For thou has holpen me who am no God,

But one, thy Brother ; heretofore a Prince,
And now a wanderer, seeking night and day
These six hard years that light—which somewhere shines
To lighten all men's darkness, if they knew !
And I shall find the light ; Yea, now it dawned
Glorious and helpful, when my weak flesh failed
Which this pure food, fair Sister, hath restored,
Drawn manifold through lives to quicken life—
Yet dost thou truly find it sweet enough
Only to live ? Can life and love suffice ?

SUJATA :

Worshipful ! My heart
Is little and a little rain will fill
The lily's cup which hardly moists the field.
It is enough for me to feel life's sun
Shine in my Lord's grace and my baby's smile,
Making the lovely summer of our home.
Pleasant my days filled with household cares
From sunrise when I wake to praise the Gods,
And give forth grain and trim the tulsi plant,
And set my handmaids to their tasks till noon,
When my Lord lays his head upon my lap
Lulled by soft song and wavings of the fan ;
And so to supper-time at quiet eve,
When by his side I stand and serve the cakes.
Then the stars light their silver lamps for sleep,
After the Temple and the talk with friends,
How should I not be happy, blessed so much ?

PRINCE :

Simple and kind ! Thou teachest them who teach.
Wiser than wisdom in thy simple lore.
Be thou content to know not, knowing thus
Thy way of light and duty ; grow, thou flower !
With thy sweet kind in peaceful shade—the light
Of Truth's high noon is not for tender leaves
Which must spread broad in other suns, and lift
In later lives a crowned head to the sky.
Excellent heart ! Learnëd unknowingly
As the dove is which flieth home by love.
In thee is seen why there is hope for man
And where we hold the wheel of life at will.
Peace go with thee and comfort all thy days !
As thou accomplishest—may I achieve.

CURTAIN.

SCENE IV

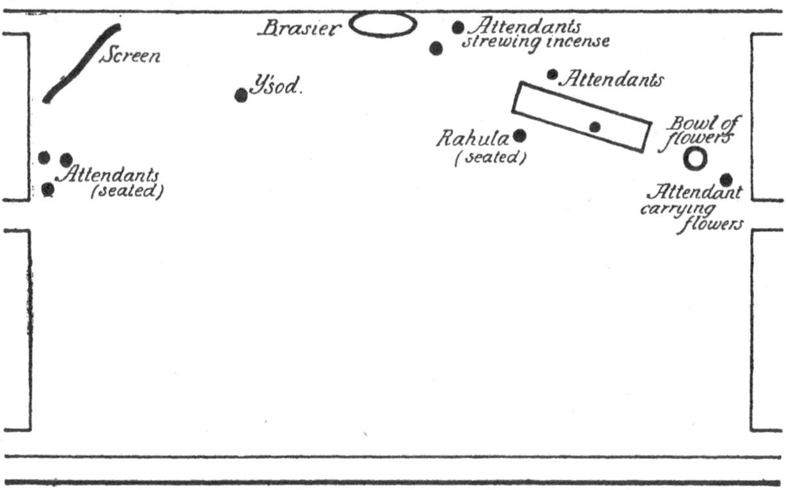

Seven years have elapsed.

SCENE : SIDDÂRTHA'S *Palace.*

YASÔDHARA ; RAHULA, *her son ;* MAIDENS.

YASÔDHARA : (*watching a flight of birds*)

Oh ! happy creatures of the wandering wing,
If ye shall light where my dear Lord is hid,
Say that Yasôdhara lives nigh to death,
For one word of his mouth, one touch of him.

(*Enter* CHITRA, *R. L. E.*)

CHITRA :

Good news ! Great Princess ! there have entered in
At the South gate merchants of Hastinpûr,
Long travelled from the sea's edge, who bring
Waved blades of gilded steel, wrought bowls in brass,
Cut ivories, spice, simples, and unknown birds,
Treasures of far-off peoples ; but they bring
That which doth beggar these, for He is seen !
Thy Lord—our Lord—the hope of all the land—
Siddârtha ! they have seen him face to face.
Yea, and have worshipped him with knees and brows
And offered offerings ; for he is become
World-honoured, holy, wonderful ; a Buddh.
And lo ! he journeyeth hither, these do say.

[*During this speech* ATTENDANTS *leave their occupation and listen attentively.*

YASÔDHARA :

Oh ! Chitra, go, call quick—call quick and bring
These merchants to my purdah, for mine ears
Thirst like parched throats to drink their blessed news.
Go bring them in—but if their tale be true,
Say I will fill their girdles with much gold,
With gems that kings shall envy : (CHITRA *exits R. L. E.*).
come ye too,
My girls, for ye shall have guerdon of this
If there be gifts to speak my grateful heart.

[ATTENDANTS *gather round* YASÔDHARA.

[*Before* MERCHANTS *enter*, YASÔDHARA *seats herself on divan with* RAHULA *at her feet*, MAIDENS *around her. Enter* CHITRA *with the* MERCHANTS TRIPUSHA *and* BHALLUK. MERCHANTS *prostrate themselves before* YASÔDHARA.

YASÔDHARA :

Ye are come
From far, fair Sirs ! and ye have seen my Lord—
Yea worshipped—for he is become a Buddh,
World-honoured, holy, and delivers men,—
And journeyeth hither. Speak ! for if this be,
Friends are ye of my House, welcome and dear.

TRIPUSHA : (*L. C.*)

We have seen thy Lord, most noble Lady—
That Sacred Master, Princess ! we have bowed
Before his feet ; for he who was lost a Prince
Is found a greater than the King of Kings.
We ourselves have heard preaching those noble Truths
His wondrous lips and done them reverence.
He cometh hither ere the first rains fall.

YASÔDHARA :

For joy—scarce can I answer. Be it well
Now and at all times with ye, worthy friends.
Take gifts and thanks. (*She signs to* CHITRA, *who gives the* MERCHANTS *her chains and rings.* YASÔDHARA *wears none herself.*) What road wendeth my Lord ?

BHALLUK: (*R. C.*)

Yogans threescore stretch from the city walls
To Rajagriha, whence the easy path
Passeth by Sona hither, and the hills.
Our oxen, treading eight slow koss a day,
Came in one moon.

(*Enter* KING SUDDHÔDANA *and* COURTIERS, *L. U. E.*

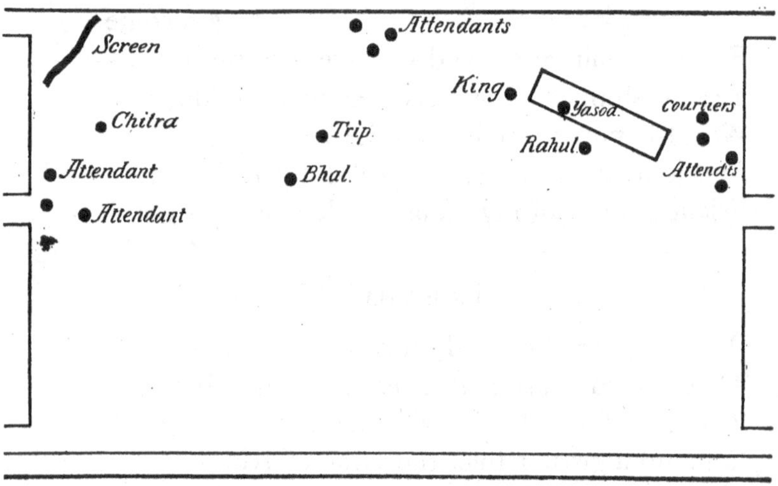

KING: (*to* COURTIERS)

Send Nobles of the Court—well-mounted lords—
Bidden to say ' I, King Suddhôdana—
Nearer the pyre by seven long years of lack—
Pray to my Son to come unto his own,
Lest I shall die and see his face no more.'
Also nine horsemen sends Yasôdhara
Bidden to say,

YASÔDHARA :

'The Princess of thy House—
Rahula's mother—craves to see thy face
As the night-blowing moon-flower's swelling heart
Pines for the moon, as pale Asôka buds
Wait for a woman's foot : if thou hast found
More than was lost, she prays her part in this,
Rahula's part, but most of all thyself.

[*Exit* CHITRA, MERCHANTS, *R. L. E.*

[MERCHANTS *prostrate themselves before they go.*

SECOND CURTAIN.

SCENE V

(*Played before second curtain.*)

SCENE: *A Road.*

(*Enter* SAGE ACHARYA *and* COURTIERS, *R. M. E.*)

SAGE: (*C. To* COURTIER)

Eager to be before—Yasôdhara
Rides in her litter to the city-walls
Where soars the bright pavilion. All around
A beauteous garden smiles—Nigrôdha named.

[*During their speeches* SAGE *and* COURTIERS *move across stage to D. L. They remain D. L. in L. corner of stage during* PRINCE'S *entrance and speech.*

FIRST COURTIER: (*R. C.*)

Outside the gates a patient folk and poor,
Whose touch for Kshatriya and priest of Brahm
Were sore defilement, do await their Prince.

SECOND COURTIER:

Yet those, too, are quick
With expectation, rising ere the dawn
To peer along the road, to climb the trees
At far-off trumpet of some elephant,
Or stir of Temple-drum; and when none comes—

(*Enter* YASÔDHARA *with* CHITRA *and* ATTENDANTS, *R. M. E.*)

YASÔDHARA: (*to* ATTENDANT)

Question ye wayfarers if any noise
Be on the road of great Siddârtha. Go!
[*Exit* ATTENDANT, *L. M. E.*

SAGE:

One slow approaches with his head close shorn,
[*Looking off*, *L. M. E.*
A yellow cloth over his shoulder cast,
Girt as the hermits are, and in his hand
An earthen bowl, shaped melonwise, the which
Meekly at each hut door he holds a space,
Taking the granted dole with gentle thanks,
And all as gently passing where none give.
Children and men and women draw behind
Into his steps, whispering with covered lips,
'Who is he? Who? When looked a Rishi thus?'

(*Enter* SIDDÂRTHA *L. M. E., in yellow robes, carrying earthen bowl, followed by* CHANNA. YASÔDHARA *stands before him, and then falls weeping at his feet.*)

YASÔDHARA:

Siddârtha! Lord!
[SIDDÂRTHA *to* YASÔDHARA, *half raising her.*

SIDDÂRTHA:

The greater beareth with the lesser love,
So it may raise it unto easier heights.

Take ye heed that no man being scaped from bonds,
Vexeth bound souls with boasts of liberty,
Free are ye rather that your freedom spread
By patient winning and sweet wisdom's skill.
I, Buddh, who wept with all my brother's tears,
Whose heart was broken by a whole world's woe,
Laugh and am glad, for there is liberty !
Ho ! ye who suffer ! know,
Ye suffer from yourselves. None else compels,
None other holds you that ye live and die,
And whirl upon the wheel, and hug and kiss
Its spokes of agony,
Its tire of tears, its waves of nothingness.
Behold I show you Truth.

[SIDDÂRTHA *raises* YASÔDHARA ; *takes her hand, and leads her off R. M. E., followed at a distance by* CHITRA *and* ATTENDANTS, *then* SAGE, CHANNA, *and* COURTIERS. *They all seem deeply moved, and whisper excitedly together. When all have made their exit, the actors should quickly take their places for the next scene behind the second curtain, the latter then rises for the last scene.*

The Return of Buddha

To face page 69]

SCENE VI

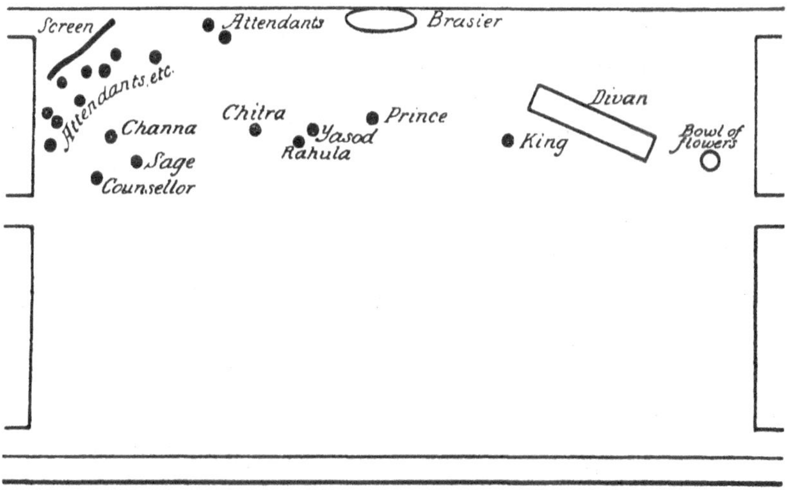

SCENE : SIDDÂRTHA'S *Palace.*

When the curtain rises the actors are just taking their places as above. An ATTENDANT *brings* RAHULA *to* YASÔDHARA. KING SUDDHÔDANA, *followed by two* ATTENDANTS *enters L. U. E. He comes forward with outstretched arms to greet* SIDDÂRTHA.

KING : (*he stands in the centre of stage ;* PRINCE *somewhat below him*)

Ends it in this
That great Siddârtha steals into his realms,
Wrapt in a clout, shorn, sandalled, craving food

Of low-borns, he whose life was a god's?
At hearing of your coming all the folk
Of white Kapilavastu and its fields
Made ready for the entrance of their Prince.
At the South gate a bright pavilion rose
With flower-wreathed pillars and the walls of silk
Wrought on their red and green with woven gold.
Also the roads were laid with scented boughs
Of neem and mango, and full mussuks shed
Sandal and jasmine on the dust; the flags
Fluttered; and on the day when you should come
It was ordained how many elephants—
With silver howdahs and their tusks gold-tipped—
Should wait beyond the ford, and where the drums
Should boom 'Siddârtha cometh!' Where the lords
Should light and worship, and the dancing girls
Where they should strew their flowers, with dance and song,
So that the steed you rode might tramp knee-deep
In rose and balsam, and the ways be fair;
While the town rang with music and high joy.
This was ordained, and all men's ears were pricked
Dawn after dawn to catch the first drum's beat
Announcing, 'Now he cometh! Siddârtha!'
My son! heir of this spacious power, and heir
Of kings who did but clap their palms to have
What earth could give or eager service bring,
Thou should'st have come apparelled in thy rank,
With shining spears and tramp of horse and foot.
Lo! all my soldiers camped upon the road,
And all my city waited at the gates;

Where hast thou sojourned through these evil years
Whilst thy crowned father mourned? and she, too, there
Lived as the widows use, foregoing joys;
Never once hearing sound of song or string,
Nor wearing once the festal robe, till now
When in her cloth of gold she welcomes home
A beggar-spouse, in yellow remnants clad.
Son! why is this?

PRINCE:

My father! thou dost know
It is the custom of my race!

KING:

Thy race.
Our race, my son, counteth a hundred thrones
From Maha Sammât, but no deed like this.

PRINCE:

The Devas know—not of a mortal line
I spake, but of descent invisible,
The Buddhas who have been and who shall be
Of these am I, and what they did I do,
And this, which now befalls, so fell before,
That at his gate a King in warrior-mail
Should meet his son, a Prince in hermit-weeds;
And that, by love and self-control, being more
Than mightiest kings in all their puissance,
The appointed helper of the worlds should bow—
As now do I—and with all lowly love

Proffer, where it is owed for tender debts,
The first-fruits of the treasure he hath brought ;
Which now I proffer.

KING :

What treasure dost thou proffer—Oh my son ?

PRINCE :

O, Amitaya ! Measure not with words
Th' Immeasurable ; nor sink the string of thought
Into the Fathomless. Who asks doth err,
Who answers, errs. Say nought !

KING :

Shall any gazer see with mortal eyes ?
Or any searcher know by mortal mind ?
[*Takes* PRINCE'S *earthen bowl from him.*

PRINCE :

Veil after Veil will lift—but there must be
Veil upon Veil behind.
Stars sweep and question not. This is enough
That life and death and joy and woe abide ;
And cause and sequence, and the course of time,
And Beings ceaseless tide,
Which, ever changing, runs, linked like a river
By ripples following ripples, fast or slow—
The same and not the same—from far-off fountain
To where its waters flow
Into the sea.

KING:

This is enough to know, the phantoms are;
The Heavens, Earths, Worlds, and changes changing them
A mighty whirling wheel of strife and stress
Which none can stay or stem.

PRINCE:

Pray not! The Darkness will not brighten! Ask
Nought from the Silence, for it cannot speak!
Vex not your mournful minds with pious pains!
Ah! Brothers, Sisters! seek
Nought from the helpless gods by gift and hymn,
Nor bribe with blood, nor feed with fruits and cakes;
Within yourselves deliverance must be sought.
Each man his prison makes.

KING: (*moves down L.*)

Each hath such lordship as the loftiest ones:
Nay, for with powers above, around, below,
Act maketh joy and woe.

PRINCE:

The devils in the underworlds wear out
Deeds that were wicked in an age gone by;
Nothing endures: fair virtues waste with time,
Foul sins grow purged thereby.
Who toiled a slave may come anew a prince
For gentle worthiness and merit won,
Who ruled a King may wander earth in rags
For things done and undone.
Higher than Indra's ye may lift your lot,

And sink it lower than the worm or gnat ;
The end of many myriad lives is this.
The end of myriads that.
Only, while turns this wheel invisible,
No pause, no peace, no staying place can be ;
Who mounts may fall, who falls will mount ; the spokes
Go round unceasingly.

What treasure do I proffer ? Those Four Truths.
Which hold all wisdom as shores shut the seas.

' *Those four truths.*' (*Music cue.*)

[*Music continues to end of scene.*

6
mf
f

dim.
p

rall.
Colla parti.
Ped.
sf

Those eight right Rules whereby who will may walk—
Monarch or slave—upon the perfect path
That hath its Stages four and Precepts eight,
Whereby whoso will live—mighty or mean,
Wise or unlearned, man, woman, young or old—
Shall, soon or late, break from the wheels of life,
Attaining blessed Nirvana.

CURTAIN.

TABLEAU.

Curtain rises immediately, showing PRINCE *alone seated in centre of stage, as at beginning of Scene III. The music should continue till after the second descent of the curtain.*

Printed by BALLANTYNE, HANSON & Co.
Edinburgh & London